Beautiful
JUNK

Creative Classroom Uses for Recyclable Materials

Karen Brackett and Rosie Manley

Fearon Teacher Aids
Simon & Schuster Supplementary Education Group

Editor: Barbara Armentrout

Copyeditor: Diane Sovljanski

Illustration: Tracy LaRue Hall

Cover painting and book design: Rose Sheifer

ISBN 0-8224-0626-8

Printed in the United States of America

Printed on Recycled Paper

Contents

PREFACE 5

SOURCES OF FREE AND INEXPENSIVE MATERIALS 6

BOXES **9**

CARDS, CATALOGS, AND OTHER PRINTED MATERIAL **16**

COFFEE CANS AND JUICE CANS **21**

EGG CARTONS **25**

FABRIC **29**

MARGARINE LIDS **34**

MILK CARTONS **36**

PAPER TUBES **41**

PLASTIC BOTTLES **46**

STYROFOAM CHIPS **49**

STYROFOAM TRAYS **53**

SUPERMARKET FLYERS **55**

VEHICLE BROCHURES **59**

WALLPAPER **62**

WOOD SCRAPS **67**

DEAR PARENTS, PLEASE SAVE FOR ME 71

MATERIALS FOR COLLAGES AND CONSTRUCTIONS 73

INDEX OF ACTIVITIES 75

 # Preface

Creative teachers use recyclable materials to enrich classroom experiences and to relate school to the child's growing knowledge of the larger environment.

Recyclable materials present a number of advantages. The most obvious advantage is the lack of expense, which allows for greater quantity and variety of materials, particularly for centers and schools that must seek alternate sources of supplies because of economic cutbacks. An equally important advantage is that recyclable materials challenge children to find unique uses for everyday objects, thereby encouraging divergent and creative thinking. Also, ecological values are communicated to children as they live and learn in a school environment where conservation of resources, multiple uses of materials, and innovative approaches are everyday practices.

We hope that this book will remind teachers (and others who work with children) about the infinite variety of free and inexpensive materials in every child's immediate environment. We also hope that this book will stimulate teachers to think creatively about new ways to provide opportunities for children to produce their own "beautiful junk."

 # Sources of Free and Inexpensive Materials

In order to obtain optimal cooperation from suppliers of "junk," we have found that it is important to

1. make personal contacts,
2. go back frequently, and
3. provide your own container for collection.

CARPET STORES

Carpet samples are often available.

FABRIC SHOPS

Scraps and remnants of ribbon and material are available. The cardboard forms that yardage (and sometimes yarn and thread) is wrapped around can also be useful.

FLORIST SHOPS

Pieces of foam, tape, foil, ribbon, and wire are available.

FRAMING STORES AND GALLERIES

Leftover pieces of matboard in a variety of interesting shapes and colors lend themselves to heavier collages.

GROCERY STORES

Boxes, boxes, boxes — and a purpose for every size. Many cardboard displays that stores dispose of are suitable for various purposes in the classroom. The produce section often yields interesting containers and separators. Also save supermarket flyers.

HOME

Your students' families can often provide dress-up clothes, including ties, shoes, hats, and jewelry. Also ask them to save such throwaways as empty food containers, paper towel rolls, empty detergent bottles, bleach bottles, old cookie sheets, buttons, yarn, scraps of material, empty egg cartons, small and tall juice cans, newspapers, magazines, and empty bottles (deodorant, shoe polish, etc.). See the suggested list, "Dear Parents, Please Save for Me. . . ," on page 71.

MILLWORK OR LUMBER COMPANIES

Wood scraps suitable for the workbench table or art center are given away by the box load. Sawdust is available, as well as fascinating curls of wood.

PRINT SHOPS

Various sizes and colors of scrap paper are available.

TILE STORES

Broken patterns of mosaic tile are usually available for a minimal charge.

WALLPAPER STORES

Wallpaper books of discontinued patterns are usually available on a first come, first served basis.

Boxes

1. ART FRAMES

Use the tops of tissue boxes to frame small pieces of art.

Variation: Collect the tops from a variety of gift boxes. Cut out the center so that it is slightly smaller than the art to be displayed.

2. BOX ANIMALS

Alligator: Use a toothpaste box for the body. Glue on paper legs, jaw, and tail.

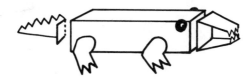

Elephant: Use a frozen-vegetable box for the body. Glue on ears, trunk, legs, and tail.

3. BOX DISPLAY CASE

To make a display case, paint or wallpaper several large, sturdy cardboard boxes. When they are dry, stack them, keeping the largest one on the bottom. Neatly tape them together.

4. BOX SORTING GAME

Let children sequence several boxes of different heights from shortest to tallest.

5. BOX TRAIN

Paint several boxes that are each large enough for a child to fit inside. Punch a hole in the front and the back of each car. Use a rope to connect the cars. Let the children use the train for imaginative play.

6. CAGES

Use a shoe box for each cage. Let children make clay animals. Also have available rocks, twigs, and sand to put in the cage. Paste strips over the open side for the bars of the cage.

7. CASH REGISTER

Glue sponge squares onto the lid of a shoe box to be the keys. Play money can be stored inside the shoe box.

8. CEREAL BOX PUZZLES

Cut the fronts of large cereal boxes into pieces (the number and complexity of the pieces will depend on the age and ability of your children). Store the pieces in a large envelope with an identical cereal box front pasted on it.

9. DOLL BED

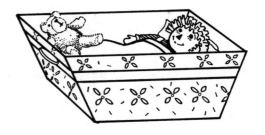

Cover a fiberboard bin (the kind with handles cut into the sides) with Con-Tact paper. Add a pillow and a blanket to the bed.

10. DOLL HOUSE

Arrange four medium-sized cartons or four shoe boxes in any desired fashion, and connect them with oversized paper clips. Let the children decorate the walls of the rooms with paint, crayons, wallpaper pieces, art paper, or Con-Tact paper. Carpet or fabric scraps make good rugs. Use small boxes, spools, wood scraps, fabric, and glue to make doll furniture. Dolls can be made from wooden ice cream spoons.

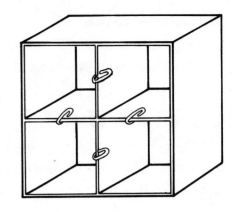

11. FEEL AND TELL BOX

Cut two squares of each of various textured items: scraps of cloth, rug samples, steel wool, sandpaper, sponges, drinking straws. Glue one of each pair of squares onto the lid of a shoe box. Glue the other pieces onto squares of cardboard, and put these squares in the box. In one end of the shoe box, cut a hole large enough for a child's hand. Put on the lid. Have each child reach inside and try to match the squares inside with the squares on the lid.

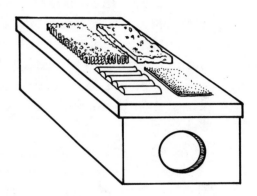

12. FELTBOARD

Cut a large box in half diagonally (see Table Easel illustration below, #24). Cut a piece of felt to fit the largest rectangular side of the box. Glue the felt to this side. Cut out felt shapes, letters, and numbers in various colors and sizes. Store the felt pieces in a shoe box.

13. GAS PUMPS

Use tall, narrow boxes, such as shovel or broom boxes. For each pump, also make a cardboard base that is slightly larger than the end dimensions of the box (see illustration). Have children paint the boxes. Add as many features as the children want. When the paint is dry, cut a hole in each pump for the hose (use a piece of an old garden hose), and glue each pump to its base.

14. GIANT BLOCKS

Tape shut the tops of heavy cardboard boxes to make giant blocks. The children will enjoy painting them.

15. IMAGINARY VEHICLES

Have children paint various sizes of boxes and glue on details made from egg carton cups, wood wheels, and plastic wrap, as well as circles made of paper, plastic, leather, wood, or cardboard.

16. "INSTANT" CAMERA

Punch a hole in each of the two narrow sides of a large baking soda box. Cut the top open. Glue construction paper over the box. Make a lens by gluing a button in the middle of one of the wide sides of the box. String a shoelace or piece of heavy yarn through the two holes and tie it securely.

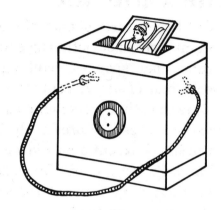

Cut out pictures in magazines and glue them to pieces of heavy tagboard that will fit inside the box. Put the pictures in the box so that the children can pull them out of the slit like photos from an instant camera.

17. LIFE-SIZED PUPPETS

Cover the front and sides of a large detergent or cereal box with cloth or paper. Draw a face on a paper plate. Glue the plate to the top of the box. For the puppet's arms and legs, cut four strips of cloth about 3" wide. Glue the arms and legs to the back of the box. Punch two holes in the top of the box to attach a cord so that the puppet can be worn on the child's chest. Rubber bands can be stapled to the ends of the arms and the legs so that the puppet can move with the child.

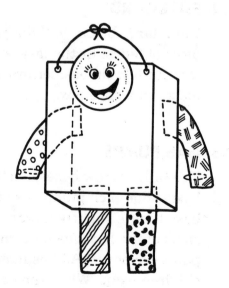

18. MASKS

For each mask, cut off the back and one end flap of a cereal box. Cover the box with paper. Cut holes for eyes, nose, and mouth. Let children decorate the masks.

19. MATH MATCHING GAME

On the side of an empty cheese box, print either the numerals 1–9 or dot arrays for those numbers. On nine clothespins, print the same set of numerals or dot arrays. Have each child try to match the clothespins with the correct numerals or dot arrays on the cheese box by clipping the clothespins on the box.

20. OUR TOWN

Show the children the large piece of heavy corrugated cardboard for the base (about 3' square) and all the boxes you have collected. Tell the children they are going to build a town. Let them decorate the boxes and the base, using paint or pieces of paper, markers, and magazine pictures. Label the buildings.

21. PUPPET STAGE

Cut off the top, bottom, and back panel of a very large cardboard box, such as one for a washing machine. Cut an opening in the top half of the front panel for the puppet stage. Decorate the box.

22. SHOPPING BASKETS

Make shopping baskets out of shoe boxes. Have the children paint their shoe boxes. Then punch two holes in each end of the box. Attach a cardboard handle with a shoelace, heavy yarn, or twine.

23. STICK PUPPETS

Glue a popsicle stick inside the front or back of a pudding box. Decorate the box.

24. TABLE EASEL

Cut a large box in half diagonally and paint it.
Use it on a table as an art easel.

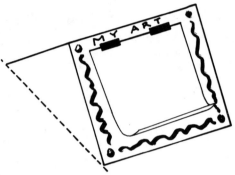

25. TALKING PUPPETS

Cover a small cereal box with plain paper. Draw a line around the box halfway between the top and the bottom. Cut along the line on the front and the sides. Fold in the back side. Draw a face on the front, or glue on facial features made with buttons, rickrack, and other small items. To make the puppet talk, put your fingers on the top and your thumb at the bottom, and pinch the box.

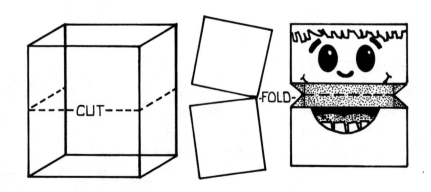

26. TELEVISION

Cut a TV-screen shape into the front of a large box. Have the children paste pictures in sequence on a long strip of paper that is the height of the "TV screen." Make two holes in the top and the bottom of the box — on either side of the screen. Put a dowel that is taller than the box into each pair of holes. Attach the ends of the strip to the dowels. The strip can be shown turning by dowels in the box (see illustration).

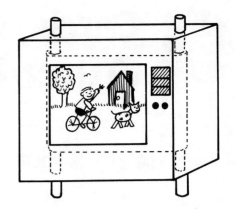

27. VALENTINE MAILBOX

Let each child paint a shoe box and decorate it by gluing on wallpaper hearts. Make a slit in the top of the mailbox for the cards and letters.

Cards, Catalogs, and Other Printed Material

Department Store Catalogs

1. HOUSES

From the household sections of the catalogs, cut pictures of bathrooms, kitchens, bedrooms, and living rooms. For the house, use paper divided into sections, a large cardboard box, or mural paper. Have the children paste on the pictures to make the different rooms in the house.

They can also use pictures from the clothing section to make paper dolls for the house. Paste the dolls on heavy paper that is folded so that it will stand up.

2. PACK YOUR SUITCASE

Use a 9" x 12" piece of construction paper for each suitcase. Have the children paste on pictures of clothing, shoes, and other items to pack. Fold the paper in half and add paper handles.

3. TRAIN SORTING GAME

Read *The Little Engine That Could*, by Watty Piper. Make an engine and four train cars from shoe boxes. Paste a picture on each car: one of clothes, one of toys, one of animals, and one of food. From catalogs and magazines, provide an assortment of pictures in each category: things we wear, things we eat, things we play with, and animals. Have the children sort the pictures into the train cars.

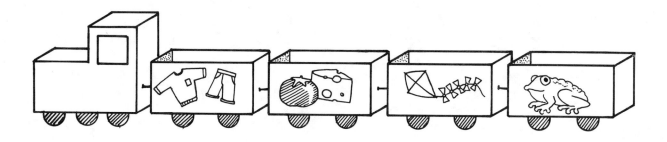

4. A TRUCKLOAD OF TOYS

Read *Big Joe's Trailer Truck,* by Joe Mathieu. Use the pattern on page 18 to make truck shapes. Cut pictures of toys from the toy section and paste them on the truck.

Holiday Cards

1. GIFT TAGS

Cut holiday cards into smaller shapes. Punch a hole in one corner, and attach the tag with yarn to a gift.

2. GREETING CARD PUZZLES

Cut large cards into several pieces (the number and complexity will depend on the age and ability of your children). Store the pieces in an envelope.

3. HOLIDAY MATCHING GAME

Cut the fronts of holiday cards in half. Place all the halves in a tray or basket. Let the children find matching pairs.

4. HOLIDAY PLACE MATS

For each place mat, children paste smaller holiday cards on a 9" x 12" piece of construction paper. Cover the front and back with clear Con-Tact paper.

5. HOLIDAY RUBBINGS

Many holiday cards have raised designs that transfer very well by rubbing. Place a card under a sheet of newsprint or thin paper and rub with the side of a thick crayon.

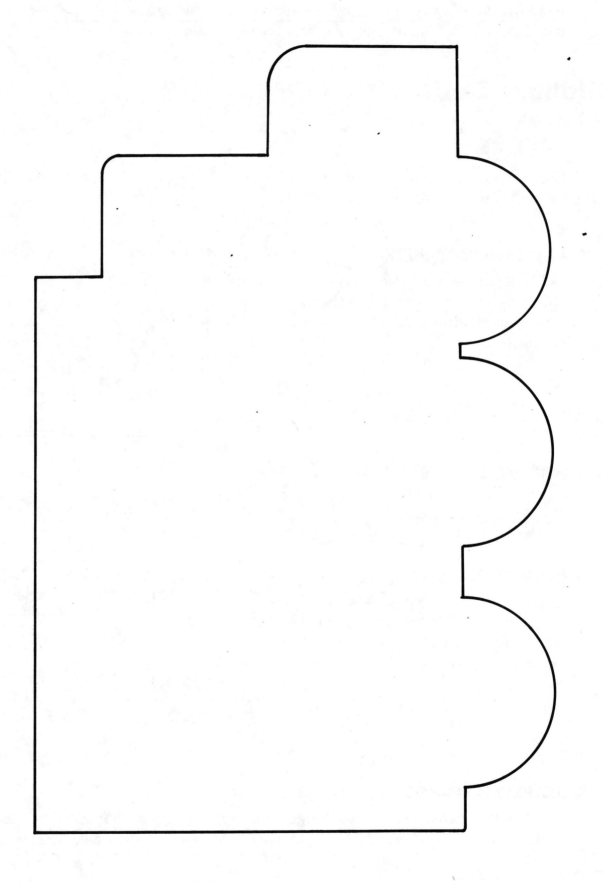

6. NEW CARDS

Paste the front of a used holiday card on a 9" x 12" piece of construction paper folded in half. Each child dictates to the teacher a message for the inside of his or her new card.

7. SALT CARDS

Choose holiday cards with winter scenes. Paint the snowy area with glue and then sprinkle it with salt. When the glue is dry, the snow will look sparkly.

8. SEWING CARDS

Choose heavyweight holiday cards. Glue the front and back together for added stability. Punch holes around the outside edge of each card. Have the children sew around the cards with yarn that has masking tape wrapped around one end as a "needle."

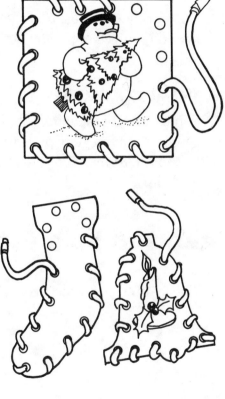

Variation: Cut cards into holiday shapes, such as a stocking, a bell, a candy cane, or a star, and proceed as above.

Junk Mail

Save old envelopes, junk mail, and magazine stamps for dramatic play about mail carriers and the post office.

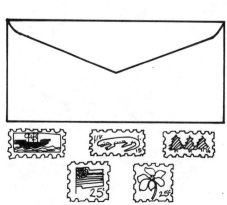

Magazines

1. ANIMAL CAGES

Cut out pictures of zoo animals. Paste them on construction paper. Cut out black stripes of construction paper and paste them over the animal pictures to make cages.

2. FACES

Cut out eyes, noses, and mouths from magazine pictures. For each child, draw an oval on a piece of paper. Let the children construct faces with the cutouts.

3. THEME COLLAGES

You can find magazines that will provide pictures for collages on just about any theme. Canvas your parents to save old issues of magazines such as *Field and Stream, Outdoor Life, Road and Track, National Geographic,* and *Better Homes and Gardens.*

Seed and Bulb Catalogs

These offer great pictures for flower collages, food collages, and color collages.

Coffee Cans and Juice Cans

1. BUBBLE MAKERS

The children can make bubbles at the water table with various sizes of cans that are open at both ends.

Variation: Add food coloring to the bubble solution.

2. DRUMS

For each drum, cut a piece of paper to fit around a coffee can. Have the children draw designs on their papers, using crayons or markers. Glue each paper around a can. Cut circles out of an old inner tube a few inches larger than the diameter of the cans. Put a rubber circle on the open end of each can. Secure the rubber circle to the can by wrapping a piece of yarn around it and knotting it tightly.

Variation: Cover the cans with Con-Tact paper instead of paper with hand-drawn designs.

3. FEELY GAME

Slip a coffee can into a large sock. Put some items inside the can. Have each child reach into the can for an item and try to identify it without looking at it.

Variation: Draw the items inside the can on a game board. Have each child reach into the can and try to find the items in the order that they appear on the game board.

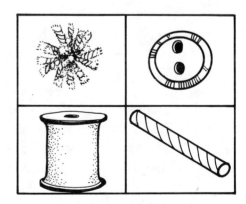

4. GARDEN POTS

For each pot, cut a piece of construction paper to fit a coffee can. Children can decorate their papers with watercolors or crayons. Then cut pieces of clear Con-Tact paper the same height as and 2" longer than the paper. Remove the paper backing from the Con-Tact paper and position the artwork face down on the sticky side, so that an inch of Con-Tact paper extends beyond each end. Attach one end of the Con-Tact paper to the side of the coffee can, wrap the paper around the can, and secure it by overlapping the other end.

Gather enough soil to fill each can half full. Add about 1 cup of water to the soil in each can, and mix it in with a spoon. Poke a hole in the soil for the plant.

Variation: Have children decorate their cans to look like faces. Plant grass seed in the cans. When the grass grows, it will look like hair.

5. GIFT CONTAINERS

• Save eggshells. Wash them thoroughly and crush them when they are dry. Have each child cover the outside of a coffee can with glue, and roll the can in the crushed eggshells. When the glue has dried thoroughly, the children can paint the cans.

• Have each child cover the outside of a coffee can with glue and then wrap colorful thick rug yarn around the can.

• Have each child cover the outside of a coffee can with Con-Tact paper. Fill the cans with popcorn, Chex Mix, or "Birdseed." (See recipes below.) Add a lid to keep the contents fresh.

Variation: *Pencil Holders.* Using plastic 12-oz. juice cans, follow any of the decorating suggestions above. Glue the can to a base for added stability.

Chex Mix

4 cups of assorted Chex cereals

Garlic powder

$\frac{1}{3}$ cup melted margarine

$1\frac{1}{2}$ cups stick pretzels

$\frac{1}{2}$ cup dry roasted peanuts

$\frac{1}{2}$ cup raisins

Spread Chex cereal out on a cookie sheet. Cover with melted margarine and sprinkle on some garlic powder. Bake at 350° for 15 minutes. Add pretzel sticks, peanuts, and raisins.

"Birdseed"

1 cup Cheerios

1 cup peanuts

1 cup Kix cereal

1 cup raisins

1 cup chocolate chips

1 cup sunflower seeds

Mix all ingredients together in a large bowl, and serve in small paper cups. This is a good take-along snack for field trips and very popular as a gift to take home.

6. GROCERY STORE PROPS

Use various cans (with the labels on) to set up a grocery store dramatic-play situation. Provide a toy cash register, play money, and paper bags to help develop concepts of stores, money, and food shopping.

7. MAGIC PAINT

For outdoor fun, take brushes and coffee cans half filled with water out to the play yard. Let children paint on cement sidewalks or walls with "magic paint."

8. PAINT CONTAINERS

Use tall plastic juice cans at the easel to hold paint.

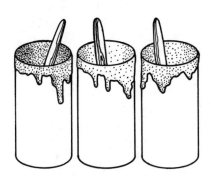

9. SEQUENCING GAME

Use five or six cans of increasing size that are open at one end. (Check the rim of each can to make sure there are no sharp edges.) Cut pieces of Con-Tact paper half an inch longer than each can. Cover each can, folding the extra paper over the rim.

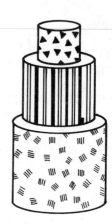

The children can practice putting the cans inside one another or arranging them from smallest to largest. They can also stack them to make towers.

10. STORAGE CONTAINERS

Cans of various sizes can be used to store materials such as beads, buttons, corks, stones, shells, cookie cutters, wooden sticks, paintbrushes, and crayons.

11. TELEPHONE

Use a hammer and nail to punch a small hole in the bottom of each of two coffee cans. Thread a long piece of nylon line through one can and tie it to a button inside the can. Do the same with the other end of the line in the other can. Have two children talk to each other on the "telephone."

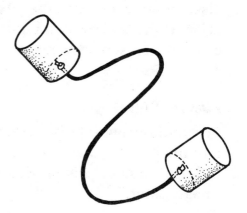

 # Egg Cartons

1. ART OBJECTS

For a unique painting experience, let the children paint cardboard egg carton cups with a variety of colors.

2. BOATS

Use the lid of an egg carton as the base of the boat. Put a small ball of clay inside the lid to hold a paper sail taped to a straw.

Variation: Use a vinyl wallpaper sail.

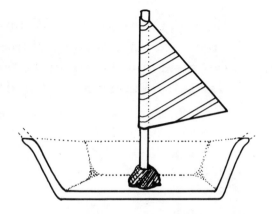

3. CARTON ANIMALS

Use cardboard egg cartons if the animals are to be painted.

Caterpillar: Cut out a strip of six egg cups to make each body. Let the children paint them. You can make feelers with pipe cleaners or by curling strips of paper around a pencil. And you can use paper hole-reinforcers for eyes.

Ant: Cut out a strip of three egg cups to make each body. Let the children paint the bodies. Add pipe cleaners or twist ties for legs and feelers.

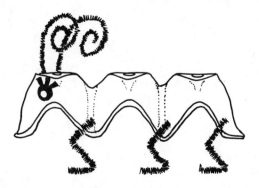

Raccoon: For each body, use three-quarters of an egg carton — both the top and the bottom. Use the flat lid for facial features. To make the nose, cut one cup from the quarter you cut off, and glue it to the head. Make the ears, tail, and paws by gluing on pieces from the lid remnant or from construction paper. After the glue is completely dry, the children can paint their raccoons.

Bunny: Use two connected cups from a styrofoam egg carton. Cut two ears from the lid and insert them into slits cut in the front cup. Add facial features and a cotton ball for the tail.

4. COLOR SORTING GAME

Paste a circle of a different color in the bottom of each cup in an egg carton. Let the children sort colored circles into the cups.

Variations: Shapes can be used instead of colors. Or the children can sort different kinds of beads, beans, or buttons.

5. EGG CARTON GAME

Glue numbers, letters, colors, or pictures of animals in the bottom of the cups in an egg carton. Have the children take turns tossing a ping-pong ball into the carton and identifying the item in the cup where the ball lands.

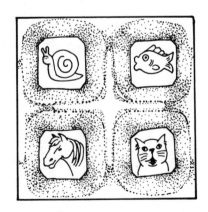

6. FLOWERS

Provide styrofoam egg cartons in a variety of colors. Cut apart the egg cups, and use one for each flower. Push a pipe cleaner through the bottom of the egg cup to make the stem. Then use scissors to cut slits toward the stem to make the petals.

Variation: Add a ball of tissue paper to the center of the flower by twisting the end of the pipe cleaner around it.

7. MIXING COLORS EXPERIMENT

Cut the bottoms of styrofoam egg cartons in half. Give each child one of these six-cup halves and put a primary color of paint in three of the cups. Let the children experiment mixing these colors in the other three cups. Then provide white paper for painting.

Variation: Give each child just two colors to mix. Read *Little Blue, Little Yellow,* by Leo Lionni. Let the children experiment mixing blue and yellow to make green.

8. PAINT SETS

Put leftover tempera paint into the cups in styrofoam egg cartons. Let the paint dry thoroughly. Then the children can use the cartons like watercolor paint sets.

9. PRINTING BLOCKS

Cut shapes from styrofoam egg carton lids. Glue each shape to a piece of wood to make a printing stamp.

Variation: Print with the bottom of a cardboard egg carton.

10. SCIENCE PROJECT: SEED GERMINATION

Use styrofoam egg cartons to germinate seeds. (Radish seeds work well.) Place a damp cotton ball in each cup. Sprinkle seeds over the cotton, and cover the egg carton with clear plastic wrap. In two or three days, you will see your seeds starting to germinate.

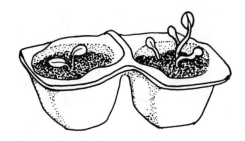

11. SCISSORS HOLDER

Spray an inverted egg carton with paint. Make a hole in each cup to hold a pair of scissors.

12. TALKING PUPPETS

Cut a styrofoam egg carton into two-cup sections. Fold each section in half so that the tops of the cups are touching. Put a fingerhole in each cup so that you can hold the puppet and make it talk. Add features.

13. TURTLES

Draw a turtle shape on heavy paper for each child. Have the children make their shells by cutting pieces of egg carton lids and gluing them on the turtles. Then the children can use markers to draw in features.

 # Fabric

Check with interior decorator stores for discarded fabric swatch books that offer a variety of patterns and textures.

1. COVERED CANS

Measure the height and circumference of each can you wish to cover. Cut a piece of fabric for each can, adding an inch to the height and the circumference measurements. Cover the cans with glue. Wrap a piece of fabric around each can, overlapping an inch around the circumference and folding the excess fabric at the top of the can over the rim for a finished look.

Twelve-ounce plastic juice containers can be used as pencil cups or gift containers.

2. DIP AND DYE FABRIC

Cut a 10" square of solid-colored fabric for each child. Put water tinted with different colors of food coloring in the four corner cups of a muffin tin. Fold the fabric square several times. Dip each corner into one of the cups of colored water, squeezing the excess liquid back into the cup. Open the fabric and let it dry.

3. FABRIC ANIMALS AND PEOPLE

From oak tag or similar heavy paper, cut a number of each of three rectangles: 4" x 6", 3" x 4", and 1" x 4". Cut a variety of fabrics in these dimensions as well. The children can make simple animals or people by gluing the basic oak tag shapes together. Then they can decorate their oak tag creations with the fabric rectangles. You might also want to provide odd-shaped fabric scraps for ears, trunks, tails, shoes, buttons, hair, and other features.

4. FABRIC COLLAGES

Offer a variety of fabric pieces cut in random sizes for collages.

Variation: Offer fabrics in only one color to produce, for example, a "blue" collage. This project can enlarge the children's concept of a color to include its various shades and hues.

5. FABRIC FLOWERS

Cut petal shapes from fabric. Glue the petals onto oak tag paper to form a flower. Add a fabric circle or a pompom in the center. Draw a stem with a crayon or a marker, and add green fabric leaves.

6. FABRIC MATCHING GAME

Cut several pairs of 2" x 4" fabric swatches. Mount each swatch on a 3" x 5" index card. Mix up the cards, and let the children find the pairs.

Variation: Cut fabric pairs in the shape of socks or mittens. After matching the pairs, the children can hang them on a clothesline.

7. FABRIC PAINTING

For a painting surface with a different texture, use solid-colored fabric at the easel instead of paper. Staple the fabric to heavy paper before painting to add stability, if necessary.

8. HAND PUPPETS

Using the pattern on page 31, cut one puppet shape out of paper for each child. Have the children decorate these shapes with fabric crayons. Then cut two puppet shapes out of solid-colored fabric for each child. Transfer the decorated puppet onto one of the cloth shapes with an iron, following the directions on the fabric crayons. Sew or glue the two fabric pieces together.

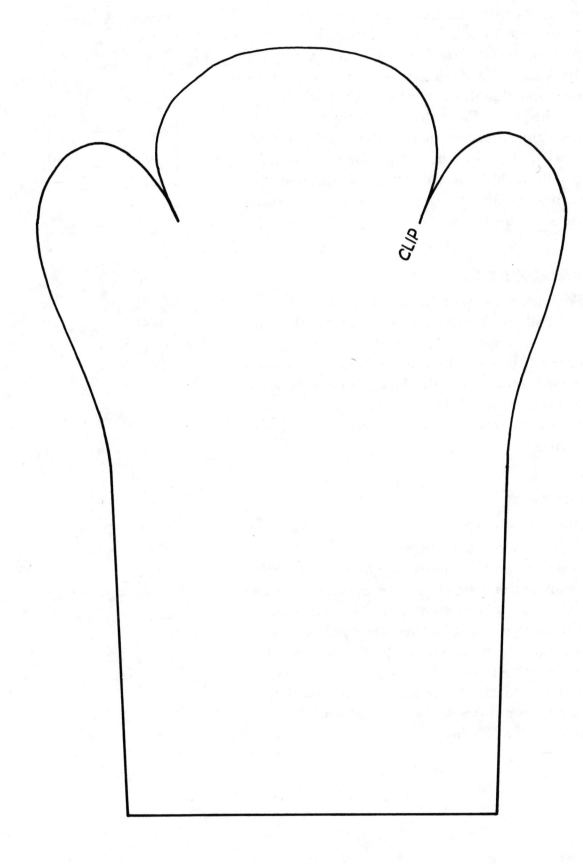

CLIP

9. MEMO PADS

For each memo pad, cut an 8" x 10" piece of corrugated cardboard. Cut two pieces of the same fabric: one 10" x 12" and one 7" x 9". Paint the front of the cardboard with glue, and center the 10" x 12" piece of fabric on it. Turn the cardboard over and glue the 1" overlap to the back for a finished edge. Paint the back of the cardboard with glue, and cover it with the 7" x 9" piece of fabric. When the glue is dry, glue a 4" x 6" note pad to the front, and punch a hole through the cardboard and the fabric so that you can attach a ribbon hanger at the top.

10. PARACHUTES

For each parachute, cut a 9" square of fabric. The children can decorate the fabric with markers or watercolors. Cut four 9" pieces of heavy string. Tie one end of each piece of string to one corner of the fabric. Tie the other ends together to a bolt or to a Fisher Price person, if available. Take the parachutes outside and toss them high in the air.

11. PILLOWS

Give each child an 11" square of paper. Have the children decorate their squares with fabric crayons. Cut two 12" squares of solid-colored fabric. Transfer the designs as in #8. Sew the squares, right sides together, on three sides. Turn the pillows right side out. Have the children help you stuff the pillows with fiberfill, and then sew the fourth side of each pillow. These pillows make wonderful one-of-a-kind gifts, and they require very little sewing skill. Maybe a parent volunteer will help?

12. "QUILTED" PLANTERS

From various fabrics, cut 1" squares with pinking shears. Paint a small area of a plastic or clay pot with glue and place fabric squares on the pot, overlapping the squares as you go. Cover the entire pot in this manner for a colorful "quilted" effect.

13. TEEPEE

Have the children decorate an old sheet with markers, fabric crayons, or paint. Drape the sheet over a card table for an instant teepee.

Variation: To make a house, decorate the sheet with windows, doors, shrubs, and so on.

14. TEXTURE MATCHING GAME

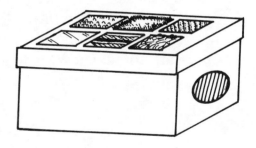

In the side of a shoe box with a lid, cut a hole large enough for a child's hand to go though. Cut several pairs of fabric swatches with distinctly different piles and textures, such as silk, flannel, corduroy, terry, and fake fur. Glue one swatch of each pair to the lid of the shoe box, and put the other swatch of each pair inside the box. Children can reach in and try to match the pairs by feeling the differences in texture.

15. WINDSOCKS

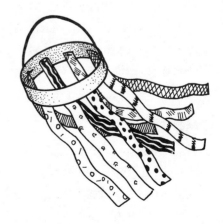

For each windsock, cut a 2" x 16" strip of heavy paper. Paste long inch-wide strips of fabric along the lower edge of the paper. Staple the ends of the paper strip together to form a circle. Attach a piece of string to the paper circle, as shown in the illustration. Children can hang their windsocks outdoors or use them as kites.

 # Margarine Lids

1. FABRIC MOBILES

Provide a variety of fabric swatches. Have each child completely paint one side of a clear plastic lid with glue and arrange fabric swatches on the lid. Punch a hole in each lid and put yarn through it for hanging.

Variation: Use tissue paper instead of fabric for a stained glass effect.

2. HOLIDAY ORNAMENTS

Cut out pictures from old holiday cards that will fit on a plastic lid. Let each child choose one and glue it on a lid. Then the children can add glitter to their ornaments. Punch a hole in each one and put yarn through it for hanging.

3. MACARONI ORNAMENTS

Have the children glue different kinds of macaroni to a plastic lid. When the glue is completely dry, spray paint the ornament gold. Add a string for hanging.

Variation: Glue a small picture of the child in the middle of the lid, and then glue macaroni around the picture. The macaroni can be painted before gluing it to the lid, if desired.

4. MOBILES

Use a large plastic lid as the base for a mobile. Punch a hole near the top to hang the mobile, and punch three or four holes around the lower edge to hang mobile items from.

34

5. NECKLACES

Children draw inside lids with permanent markers. Punch a hole through each lid and string it on a piece of yarn long enough to fit over a child's head.

6. PLAYDOUGH BIRTHDAY CAKES

Children fill plastic lids with playdough. Use real candles—or sticks or straws.

Variation: *Playdough 3-D Collages.* Fill the lids with playdough. Then the children can press collage materials into the dough. Items that work well include beans, colored stones, pine needles, acorns, rice, and macaroni.

7. RING TOSS GAME

Cut the center out of plastic lids to make hoops. Use the hoops for a ring toss game.

8. STENCILS

Cut a square, a rectangle, a triangle, or a circle out of the middle of margarine lids. Tape each lid to a piece of paper. Have each child dip a sponge in tempera and dab inside a shape until it is completely filled in. Lift the lids off carefully.

Variations: Use holiday shapes to make wrapping paper.

The shapes that have been cut out of the lids can also be traced around or used for rubbings.

9. WATER PLAY TOYS

Children can float plastic people or animals in plastic lids in the water play table.

Milk Cartons

1. BARNS

For each barn, cut a milk carton in half. Paint the top half with tempera that has a small amount of liquid soap in it. Cut flaps in front for the doors. Fold 2" x 4" tabs of stiff paper in half, and have the children draw or paste pictures of animals on them to go inside the barn.

2. BIRD FEEDERS

Cut two "windows" on opposite sides of a milk carton. Make a hole under each window and put a twig or dowel through both holes for the perches. Make a small hole in the top of the carton and attach a string so that it can hang from a tree branch. Fill the feeder with birdseed and hang it outside for the birds to enjoy!

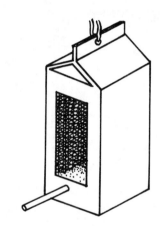

3. BOATS

Cut a half-gallon carton in half lengthwise. Lay one half on its side for the base of the boat. Put a wad of clay inside to hold a paper sail taped to a straw.

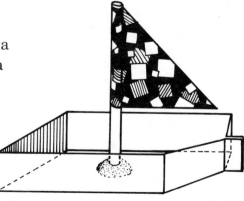

4. BOWLING PINS

Use half-gallon cartons as bowling pins. They stand up well when children are setting them up, and they make very little noise when they are knocked down.

5. BUILDING BLOCKS

To make heavy building blocks, fill various sizes of milk cartons with sand. Tape the tops flat.

6. DOLL HOUSE

Cut away one side of a half-gallon milk carton. Paste colored paper or wallpaper inside. You can make a two-story house by adding a shelf. You can also cut out windows for added interest. This house is a perfect size for Fisher Price people!

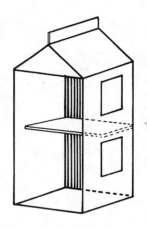

7. EASTER BASKETS

Cut a milk carton in half. Cover the bottom half with decorated paper, wrapping paper, or tissue paper. Poke holes in opposite sides and attach a pipe-cleaner handle. Fill the basket with Easter grass.

8. GARAGES

Cut a door in the front of several half-gallon milk cartons. Cover each carton with a different color of paper. Children can match colored cars to the appropriately colored garage.

Variation: Cover all the garages with the same color of paper and put a different number on each one. Children can match numbered cars to numbered garages or put the appropriate number of cars in each garage — for example, three cars in Garage Number 3. The same concept can be used with letters and shapes as well.

9. HOLLOW BLOCKS

Cut the tops off two milk cartons of the same size. Push one inside the other, top first, to make a sturdy, hollow block. The blocks can be covered with Con-Tact paper to add interest.

10. PAINT CONTAINERS

For a disposable paint container that will fit in most easel trays and will hold long easel brushes, cut the top off a quart or half-gallon carton.

11. PLANT CONTAINERS

Cut the top off a milk carton and use the base as a plant container. Decorate it or cover it with a watercolor painting or a crayon drawing if the plant is to be a gift.

For a long planter, cut the carton in half lengthwise and lay it on its side so that it can accommodate two or three plants.

12. SHAKERS

Fill pint cartons with a small amount of rice or some buttons or small stones. Tape the tops closed and use the shakers for musical instruments.

13. SIMPLE HOUSES

For each house, cut a milk carton in half. Cover the bottom half with construction paper, and paste on paper rectangles and squares for doors and windows. Have the children draw members of their families on tongue depressors and place them in their houses.

14. SOUND MATCHING GAME

Fill pairs of pint containers with the same thing, such as rice, bells, a penny, dried beans, or marbles. Tape the tops closed, and mix the cartons around. Have the children shake the cartons and find the pairs that sound the same.

15. STORAGE CONTAINERS

Cut the tops off half-gallon cartons, and use the bottoms to store small items, such as buttons and little people. So that the contents can be identified at a glance, cover each container with paper and "label" it with a picture of the item stored inside.

16. TELEVISION

Cut a window in the front of a half-gallon carton. Cut a vertical slit in each side. Have children draw sequences of pictures on long strips of paper, such as adding machine paper. Thread the paper through the slits, and pull it through slowly to watch the "show."

17. TRAFFIC LIGHTS

For each traffic light, cover a quart milk carton completely with black paper. Cut red, yellow, and green circles and have children paste them in the appropriate places. Add string to the top so that the children can hang them outside and play "traffic games" with their tricycles and Big Wheels.

18. VALENTINE MAILBOXES

Cut half-gallon cartons as shown in the illustration. Decorate each one with hearts and the child's name in large print. Hang the boxes with thumbtacks, and let the children deliver their valentines.

19. WEIGHT GUESSING GAME

Fill cartons with different amounts of material, and have the children arrange them in order of weight. Have scales available so that the children can verify their guesses.

 # Paper Tubes

1. BINOCULARS

For each pair of binoculars, tape two identical short tubes together. Add a string for a neck strap.

Variation: Cover the ends of the tubes with colored cellophane.

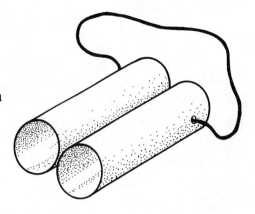

2. BIRD FEEDERS

For each bird feeder, punch two equidistant holes near one end of a short tube. Cover the tube lightly with peanut butter. Roll the tube in birdseed, or place it in a plastic bag with the birdseed and shake the bag to cover the tube with seeds. Slip a string through the two holes and knot it. Hang the bird feeder from a tree branch during the winter to help our feathered friends!

3. BUILDING "BLOCKS"

Provide various sizes of tubes in the block area to add interest to block buildings. Tubes can be used as towers, and they can be decorated with markers to add detail. Children also enjoy labeling various aspects of their constructions with paper signs, such as "Rocket Launch."

4. CARDBOARD VEHICLES

For toy cars, trucks, and train cars, slice tubes and use the rings for wheels on bodies made from cartons.

5. COLLAGES

Slice tubes into rings of various widths. Leave some rings intact, and slice others to "open" them. Have the children glue the tube pieces to heavy tagboard. Encourage them to build vertically as well as horizontally to achieve a 3-D effect. The collages can be painted for added interest.

6. DESK ORGANIZERS

Each child paints or covers four tubes of different lengths with paper. Then the four tubes are glued together onto a circular cardboard base. This desk organizer can hold pencils, rulers, and pens.

7. KAZOOS

For each kazoo, have the children decorate a tube with crayons or paint. Punch a hole near one end. Cover that end with waxed paper, and hold the paper in place with a rubber band. Hum into the open end.

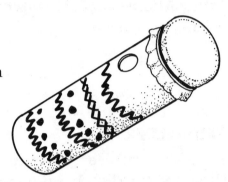

8. MARACAS

For each maraca, have the children decorate a tube. Pinch one end flat and staple it closed. Put some rice or small stones in the tube. Staple the other end, add a few felt or cloth streamers, and shake, shake, shake!

9. MICROPHONES

To make a microphone, glue an egg carton cup to the end of a tube. Add a piece of string or yarn to represent the wire.

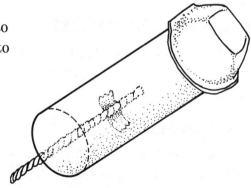

10. MOBILES

Use a tube as the base of a mobile. Attach objects to pieces of string, and tape the strings to the tube.

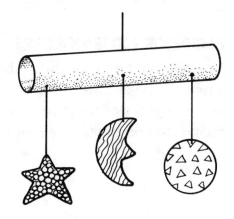

11. NECKLACES

Slice tubes into rings that are an inch or two wide. Have the children paint the rings. When the paint is dry, they can string the rings on yarn to make necklaces.

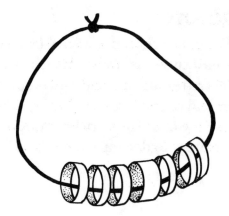

12. PLAYDOUGH ROLLING PINS

Use tubes to smooth and flatten playdough.

Variation: Glue yarn, beans, rice, or other small objects to tubes to produce imprints in the playdough.

13. PUPPETS

For each puppet, use a tube as the body. Provide circles and rectangular pieces of paper that the children can use for faces and limbs. To further enhance the creations, offer felt pieces, buttons, scraps of material, paper scraps, and yarn.

14. RECIPE OR NOTE HOLDERS

For each holder, decorate a tube, glue one end to a heavy circular base, and cut two equidistant slits in the top of the tube so that it can hold a recipe card or a note.

15. ROBOTS

For each robot, use a shoe box as the body and small tubes as limbs. Attach the tubes to the box by flattening one end and stapling it to the side or end of the box (see illustration). Provide a variety of buttons, rickrack, foil scraps, and pipe cleaners to decorate the robots.

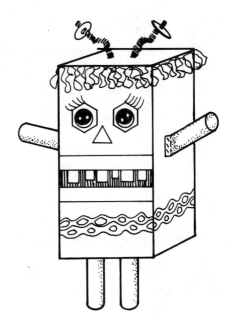

16. ROCKETS

For each rocket, cut two equidistant slits in one end of a paper towel tube. Have the children paint their tubes. Slip a foil-covered paper triangle into the slits for the rocket's nose.

Variation: Glue an egg carton cup over one end of the tube (do not slit the end) for the rocket nose.

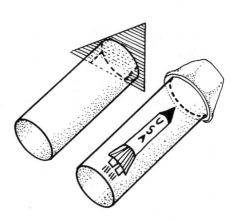

17. SAND PLAY TOYS

As interesting additions to the sand, rice, or cornmeal table, use tubes of various lengths as funnels and containers.

18. SNAKES

Have each child paint four or five short tubes and string them together to make a snake. Allow enough string for a long handle so that the children can pull their snakes along the floor and watch them wiggle.

19. TUBE ART

Have children paint tubes with a variety of colors. You can add salt or sand to the paint for a textured surface. Tubes can also be used as unique bases for collages. (See Materials for Collage and Construction, pages 72–73, for suggested materials.)

20. VASES

For each vase, decorate a tube, and glue one end to a heavy circular base. Put pipe-cleaner-stemmed paper flowers in it.

21. VEHICLE PLAY PROPS

Use tubes for tunnels, garages, subways, and covered bridges to enhance imaginary play with small cars and trucks.

 # Plastic Bottles

1. DIGGER

Use a liquid laundry detergent bottle with a handle for this project. An adult cuts the bottle with a craft knife, according to the illustration. This makes a sturdy "digger" for the sandbox or cornmeal table. If you remove the plastic cap, the digger becomes a funnel.

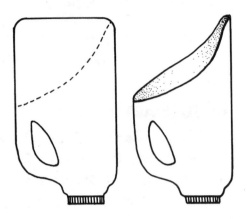

2. DRAMATIC PLAY PROPS

Save a variety of plastic bottles to use in the classroom's housekeeping area or when you set up a grocery store for a dramatic play situation.

3. FUNNEL

Any plastic bottle with a narrow neck can be used (salad oil bottle, 1-liter soda bottle, detergent bottle, 1-quart milk or juice bottle). Wash the bottle thoroughly and cut off the bottom. Invert the bottle to use it as a funnel.

4. PAINT "ROLLERS"

Save roll-on deodorant bottles that have easily removable roller tops. Wash them thoroughly and fill them with tempera paint. Replace the roller tops, and let children enjoy rolling the paint onto their papers. To store them, put the caps back on.

So DRY!

5. PLASTIC CANDLEHOLDERS

An adult cuts the tops off plastic soda bottles about 6 inches down and trims the edges with a sharp pair of scissors. This is necessary so that the base of each candleholder will be even. Provide glue and materials to decorate the holders, such as ribbons, stickers, glitter, and holiday cutouts. Add a candle to complete each holder.

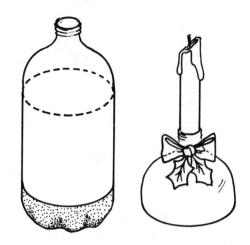

6. SCIENCE PROJECT: WATER PRESSURE EXPERIMENT

Study changes in water pressure by adding water to a container that has a hole in it. By changing the water height and adding holes to the bottle, you can demonstrate concepts about water pressure.

Try a container with one hole first. What happens to the force of the water coming out of the hole as the water level gets lower?

Then add a second hole and observe. Does the water come out of both holes at the same speed? Add a third hole and continue the observations.

The scientific concept demonstrated in this experiment is that the velocity of the water is directly related to the height of the water level above a given hole. The higher the water above the hole, the greater the water pressure.

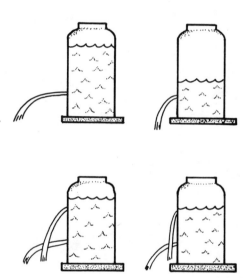

7. SODA BOTTLE TERRARIUM

An adult cuts the neck off a 2-liter plastic soda bottle with a craft knife and then removes the label and the opaque plastic bottom (hot water in the bottle makes the bottom come off easier). Place potting soil in the opaque bottom of the container. Arrange plants, rocks, and figures in the soil. Water well. Invert the clear plastic top and push it into the opaque bottom to make a domed top. Glue on a bow for decoration.

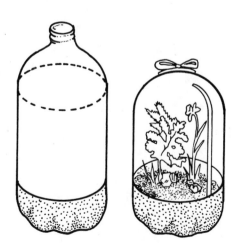

Note: You can use the top part of the bottle as a funnel in the water table or the sandbox. Tape the cut edge of the bottle neck.

Styrofoam Chips

1. CATERPILLARS

Read *The Very Hungry Caterpillar,* by Eric Carle. Have the children paste green chips along a popsicle stick to make a caterpillar puppet (to color chips, see #3). Add features with markers, and use short pieces of pipe cleaner for the antennas.

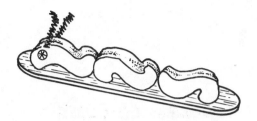

2. CHRISTMAS TREES

For each child, cut a Christmas tree shape from green construction paper. Then the children can break chip pieces apart and paste them in rows on the tree to resemble popcorn chains. Provide colored foil scraps to be pasted on as ornaments.

3. COLORED CHIPS

Fill a clean coffee can about three-quarters full with styrofoam chips. Add a small amount of tempera to the can. Cover the can and shake it vigorously until the pieces are coated with paint. Spread them out on newsprint to dry. These make colorful collages and sculptures.

Variation: Chips can also be colored by shaking them with paint in a ziploc bag.

4. FACE COLLAGES

For each collage, draw a large circle on heavy paper. The children can use styrofoam chips to represent facial features. This is even more fun if you offer a variety of chips of different shapes.

5. IGLOOS

For each igloo, cut a small doorway in an inverted margarine tub. The children can then glue chips over the entire surface.

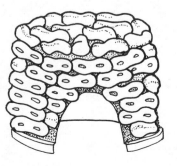

6. INCHWORMS

Read *Inch by Inch,* by Leo Lionni. Have the children paint paper tubes brown to resemble tree trunks, and paste chips on the sides to represent inchworms.

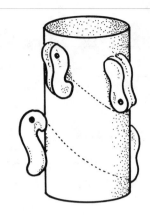

7. NUMBER COLLAGES

For each number collage, divide a heavy paper base into five sections and number them. Have the children paste the appropriate number of chips in each section.

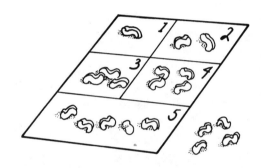

8. POPCORN

Read *Popcorn,* by Frank Asch. Cut a large pot from black construction paper (see the pattern on page 51). Paste it on a larger sheet of paper. Paste chips on the pot to represent the popcorn.

9. PUSSY WILLOWS

The children draw branches with cotton swabs dipped in black paint. Then they paste on pieces of chips to represent pussy willow blossoms.

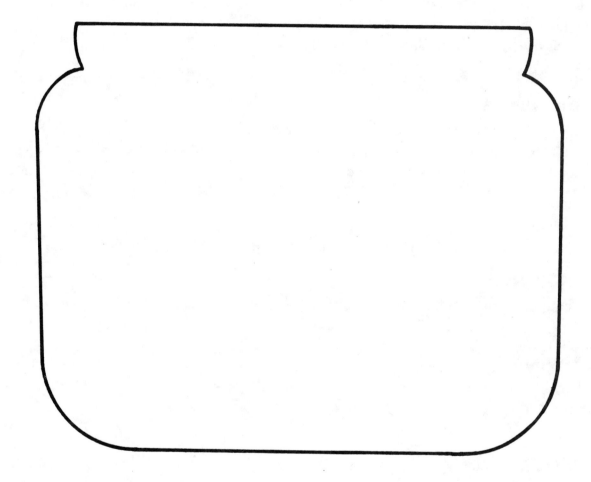

10. SCULPTURES

For each sculpture, use heavy cardboard or a large piece of styrofoam as the base. Have the children build sculptures with chips and toothpicks. The sculpture is sturdier if the toothpicks are dipped in glue before being inserted in the chips. Encourage the children to build vertically as well as horizontally.

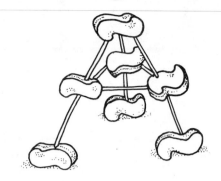

11. SHAPES

On heavy paper, draw the outline of a circle, a square, a triangle, a diamond, or an oval. Have the children paste chips along the outline of the shape.

Variation: Use the child's first initial. With older children, use the entire name.

12. SNOWBALLS

For each child, draw a 4" circle on heavy paper. Then the children can glue chips close together inside the circle to make textured "snowballs."

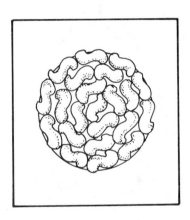

13. SNOW NECKLACES

Make holes in styrofoam chips. Have the children string the chips on yarn.

14. SPARKLY COLLAGES

Have the children glue chips onto heavy paper. Then they can paint the chips with glue and sprinkle them with glitter.

15. TEXTURE WALK

Place several plastic dish pans in a row on the floor. Fill each one with one type of textured material, such as fur, styrofoam chips, sand, or old playdough. Have children remove their shoes and socks and step from pan to pan, discussing how each feels and sounds. (Young children may need to hold someone's hand as they step from one pan to another.)

16. WATER PLAY TOYS

Provide chips as well as larger pieces of foam at the water play table.

 # Styrofoam Trays

1. ART SUPPLIES

Use trays as bases for collages or as paint pans.

2. BEACH PICTURES

Have the children glue sand and shells to styrofoam trays. Provide markers so that they can add details.

3. FINGERPAINT PRINTS

Place one or two colors of fingerpaint on each tray, and have the children spread the paint on their trays. When each painting is completed, carefully place a piece of newsprint over it. Press gently and smoothly and then lift off the print.

4. MONOPRINTS

For each monoprint, cut off the edges of a styro-foam tray. Have each child draw a design or a picture on the smooth side of a tray, pressing hard with a pencil or ballpoint pen. Cover the tray with paint. Carefully lay a piece of paper over the painted surface, and smooth it with your hand. Carefully pull off the paper.

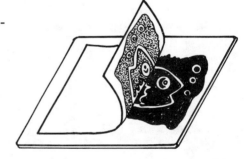

Variation: Make holiday cards, using monoprints.

5. SEWING CARDS

Wash and dry trays well. Thread plastic needles with yarn, and let the children push them in and out of the trays, forming interesting designs.

Variation: Children can thread buttons, fabric, or macaroni onto the yarn as they go.

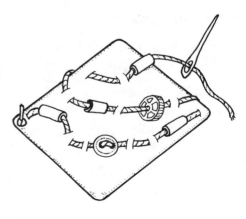

6. SHIPS

For each ship, glue a styrofoam egg carton lid to the tray. If you wish, cut out windows before gluing. Next, glue on an egg carton bottom with the egg cups up. Attach spools or plastic container tops for smoke stacks.

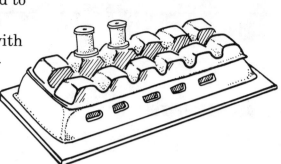

7. SORTING TRAYS

Use four trays. Label each one with a picture of a different kind of macaroni: elbow, ziti, wagon wheel, rigatoni. Let children sort real macaroni into the appropriate trays.

Variation: Use different kinds of nuts, beans, or seeds.

8. STYROFOAM PRINTING STAMPS

Cut a styrofoam tray into various shapes, designs, or patterns. Glue each piece onto the end of a dowel or a small block of wood for easy handling. Allow the stamps to dry at least overnight. The children can press the styrofoam shapes into an ink pad or dip them into tempera paint and then print a design on paper.

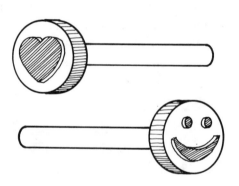

9. TRAYS FOR ART MATERIALS

For art projects that call for several materials, use styrofoam trays to organize the materials so that they are easily accessible.

10. YARN WEAVING

Cut off the edges of the trays. Make ½"-long slits around the edges of each tray. Slip a long piece of yarn, knotted at one end, into one of the slits. Have the children weave the yarn in and around the slits to produce interesting designs.

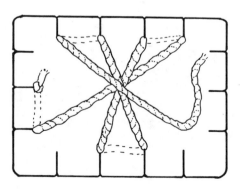

Supermarket Flyers

1. CONCENTRATION

Cut 2" x 3" cards from heavy paper. Paste matching food pictures on the cards, making as many pairs as desired. Start by having the children match the cards face up. Then proceed to the conventional Concentration game with the cards face down.

2. FAVORITE FOODS COLLAGES

Have each child paste pictures of his or her favorite foods on a paper plate.

Variation: Trace around each child on a large piece of newsprint. Have the children paste pictures of their favorite foods within their body outlines.

3. FISHING GAME

Make a fishing pole from a dowel or a long paper towel tube. Tie a magnet to one end of a string, and tape the other end of the string to the pole. Paste food pictures on heavy paper pieces, and put a paper clip on each piece. The children can fish for food pictures. You can also ask them to fish for a particular color of food or for a food in a particular food group.

4. FOOD DOMINOES

Draw a line down the middle of heavy 2" x 4" cardboard rectangles. Paste pairs of food pictures randomly on the game pieces. Play food dominoes the same as regular dominoes, but match foods instead of numbers of dots.

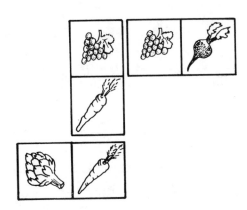

5. FOODS SORTING GAME

The children can sort the game pieces from the Lotto game (# 8) or the Concentration game (# 1). They can sort the food pictures by color or by food group. Add some nonedible grocery store items, such as soap or paper products, so that they can also sort the pictures into edible and nonedible categories.

6. FOODS MATCHING GAME

On a large piece of heavy paper (approximately 9" x 12"), paste a series of food pictures in a column on the left-hand side of the paper. Paste a matching set of pictures in a different order on the right-hand side of the paper. Cover the paper with clear Con-Tact paper. Have children draw lines connecting the matching food pictures, using a water-based marker. Wipe the game clean with a wet tissue before the next child uses it.

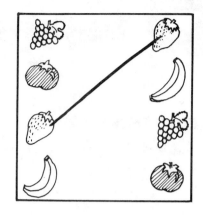

7. GROCERY MURAL

As a classroom project, draw shelves, a produce area, and meat area on a large piece of newsprint. Have the children paste pictures of grocery items in the appropriate areas.

Variation: Draw kitchen storage places, such as cupboards, a refrigerator, and a table, on which the children can paste food pictures.

8. LOTTO GAME

Obtain several copies of the same flyer. Make individual game boards from heavy paper. Divide each one into six sections. Paste a picture of a food item in each section. Make a corresponding single game piece for each picture on the game board. Have the children match the playing pieces to the food pictures on the game boards. Cover the game boards and the pieces with clear Con-Tact paper for durability.

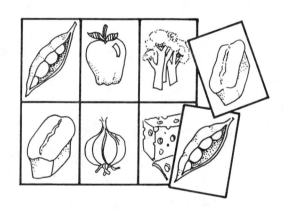

9. NUMBER COLLAGES

Cut out the numbers in food prices for number collages.

Variation: Cut out letters and words for letter collages.

10. SHOPPING CARTS

Cut shopping carts from construction paper (see the pattern on page 58). Have the children paste grocery cutouts onto the cart.

11. SHOPPING LISTS

Paste food pictures on cards, and print the name of the food on its card. Provide the children with paper and pencils so that they can copy the food words to make shopping lists.

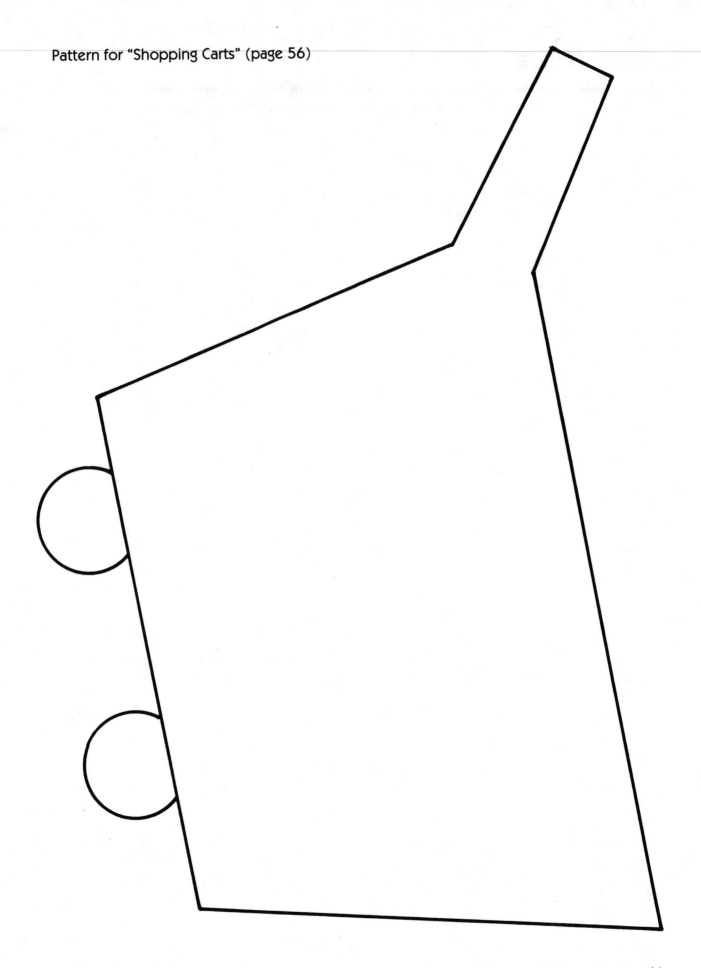

# Vehicle Brochures

Collect brochures from car, boat, motorcycle, recreational vehicle, and airplane dealers for the following activities. When you visit showrooms, mention your purpose. Dealers often have outdated brochures to donate.

Whenever you are working with pictures, use them to talk about size, color, shape, and number. "How many wheels does it have? Which one has more wheels? What color is it?"

1. PICTURE BOOKS

Paste pictures of vehicles onto construction paper. The pages can be stapled into a book or put into a binder. Each child can make his or her own book, or the class can collaborate on one large book for the book corner.

Variation: Large brown grocery bags can be cut into sheets and stapled together to serve as pages for your book.

2. STORY STARTERS: "MY TRIP"

Have each child choose a vehicle picture and paste it onto a piece of paper. Then each child dictates a story to the teacher about a real or imaginary trip he or she took in that vehicle.

3. "THINGS THAT GO" COLLAGE

Put up a large sheet of paper or newsprint entitled "Things That Go." Have the children cut out and paste pictures of various methods of transportation on the paper.

4. TRANSPORTATION GAMES

Lotto games, domino games, and matching games can be made with small pictures from these flyers.

Variation: After the children have found the pairs, show them two matching pictures and one different picture together. Ask them to point to the one that is different.

5. TRANSPORTATION MURAL

As a classroom project, do a transportation mural. It can include all aspects of transportation or just one, such as water travel or air travel. Children can paste appropriate vehicles in place and add detail with markers or crayons.

6. TWO-DIMENSIONAL TOY VEHICLES

The children can paste pictures of vehicles onto heavy paper that is folded to stand up. Use the pictures in the block area to enhance imaginary play.

7. TYPES-OF-TRAVEL SORTING GAME

Set up trays or pockets made of large envelopes, labeled pictorially as water, air, land, and space. Have the children sort pictures of vehicles according to where they travel.

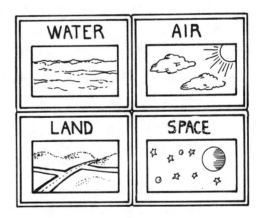

8. VEHICLE MOBILES

Mount pictures of vehicles on heavy paper. Hang the pictures on strings from a base such as a paper towel tube. Each mobile can show a variety of modes of transportation, or it can show just one, such as water travel.

Variation: Hang pictures of air travel vehicles from the ceiling.

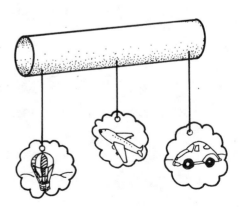

9. VEHICLE PUZZLES

Paste large pictures of vehicles on heavy paper. Cut each picture apart (the number and complexity of the pieces will depend on the age and ability of your children). Store the pieces in a large envelope that has the same vehicle picture, uncut, on the front.

Wallpaper

1. CHAMELEONS

Read *A Color of His Own,* by Leo Lionni. Have each child glue four squares (each about 4½" x 6") of different patterns of wallpaper onto a 9" x 12" piece of construction paper. Punch a hole in the corner of the paper. Cut out chameleons from stiff clear plastic (see pattern on page 63). Punch a hole in the tail of each chameleon, and attach one to each child's paper with a piece of yarn. Children can see their chameleons change colors as they move them from one pattern of wallpaper to another.

2. CHICKS IN EGGS

The children each paste two yellow circles for the chick on a piece of paper and make features with markers. Then they each cut out a wallpaper egg and cut the egg in half. They attach the egg halves to the paper with a brass fastener so that the egg opens and closes to uncover the chick.

3. COLOR COLLAGES

Designate certain days as color days. On "Red Day," for example, provide pieces of wallpaper with red in them for making collages.

4. FISH

Cut wallpaper into 3" x 12" strips. About 2 inches from one end of each strip, cut a slit halfway from the top. About 2 inches from the other end, cut a slit halfway from the bottom. Use the slits to connect the strip. Add features.

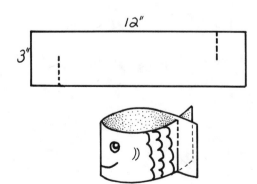

5. MEMO PADS

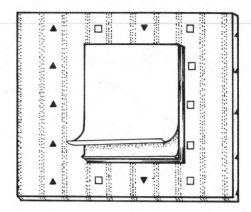

Cover a square piece of heavy cardboard with wallpaper. Glue a memo pad to the center of the wallpaper.

Variation: Cut the cardboard into a shape, such as a teapot, a watermelon, or a pineapple.

6. PAJAMAS

Read *Ira Sleeps Over,* by Bernard Waber. Cut out matching pajama tops and bottoms from wallpaper (see pattern on page 65). Have children find a matching pair and glue the top and bottom on a piece of paper. Have markers available so that the children can draw in head, hands, and feet. If desired, you can also cut teddy bears from brown paper for the children to glue onto their pictures.

7. PAPER CHAINS

Cut wallpaper into strips. Have children glue the strips together to make paper chains.

8. PATTERN DOMINOES

Cut two 2" x 2" squares from each of twelve different patterns of wallpaper. Cut twelve 2" x 4" rectangles out of heavy cardboard. Draw a line on each rectangle to divide it into two 2" x 2" squares. Paste the wallpaper squares randomly onto the rectangles.

To begin playing, place one domino in the center. Then take turns adding dominoes that match.

9. PATTERN MATCHING GAME

Use a marker and ruler to divide a large piece of tagboard into eight sections. Cut two pieces from each of eight different patterns of wallpaper. The pieces should be the same size as the sections on the tagboard. Glue one set of pieces to the tagboard. Have the children match the other set of pieces to the sample.

Variation: Put the matching game in a spiral notebook.

Pattern for "Pajamas" (page 64)

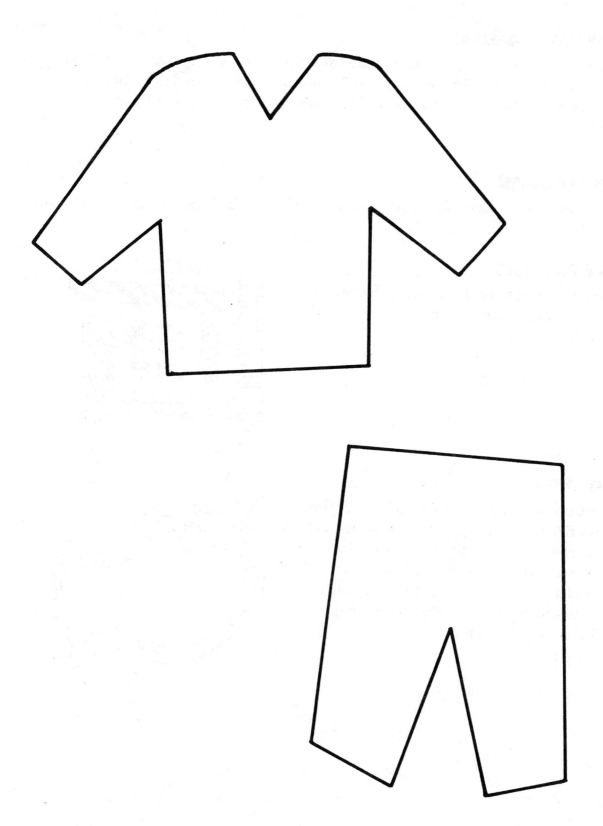

10. PENCIL HOLDERS

Have the children cover juice cans with wallpaper. These can be used for gifts.

Variation: Cover coffee cans with wallpaper for canisters or plant holders.

11. RAINY DAY UMBRELLAS

Cut out an umbrella shape and a handle from each of several patterns of wallpaper. Have the children find matching umbrellas and handles and glue them on paper. Provide markers so that the children can draw people under their umbrellas.

12. STRIP COLLAGES

Cut a variety of strips of wallpaper. Let the children do collages, using these strips.

13. STRIPE COLLAGES

Provide pieces of striped wallpaper. Have the children arrange these pieces as they like and glue them on paper.

14. STUFFED FISH

Cut out two wallpaper fish for each child. Hold the two fish together, and punch holes an inch or two apart around the edge of the fish. Have each child sew the two halves of a fish together with yarn and a plastic needle until it is almost completely joined. Stuff the fish with newspaper, and finish sewing around it.

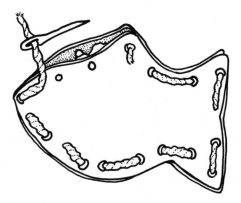

66

 # Wood Scraps

1. BOATS

Children can build their own boats by nailing pieces of wood together with flat-head nails. The top piece of each boat should be somewhat smaller than the bottom piece. The boats can be decorated with permanent markers. A fabric scrap, glue, and a dowel makes a great sail.

2. GEOBOARDS

Give each child a piece of wood. Let the children hammer flat-head nails into their pieces of wood in a random fashion. Then they make patterns by spreading colored rubber bands over the nail heads.

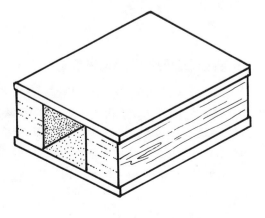

3. MUSICAL INSTRUMENTS FROM WOOD

Sandpaper Blocks: Cut wood scraps from a 1 x 4 into pieces that measure 1" x 2" x 4". Sand down all rough edges. Cut sandpaper into 4" x 6" pieces. Wrap a piece of sandpaper around each block, and secure it with thumbtacks. Add a small sanded block of wood or a drawer pull for a handle. To play the blocks, rub two of them together.

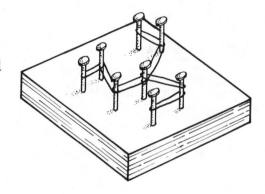

Tone Blocks: For each tone block, cut two pieces of ¼" plywood into 4" x 5 ½" rectangles, and cut two 1"-wide strips from a 1 x 6 piece of lumber. Assemble the wood pieces with glue and small nails according to the illustration. To play the tone block, strike it with a small wooden hammer or a dowel.

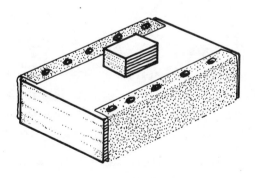

4. PRINTING BLOCKS

Small wood blocks make great bases for printing stamps. Cut shapes from styrofoam trays or pieces of rubber, and glue a shape to each base. Allow the glue to dry thoroughly. Then the children can press the shapes into a sponge saturated with tempera paint and print onto paper.

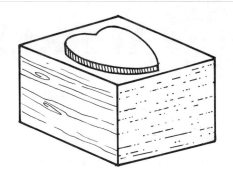

5. TEXTURE PAINT

Mix $\frac{1}{3}$ cup sawdust with $\frac{2}{3}$ cup tempera paint.

6. WALKIE-TALKIES

Use a wood block for the base of each walkie-talkie. Have each child draw a speaker, buttons, and other features on it with a marker. For the antenna, attach a straw to the side of the wood block with a heavy-duty stapler.

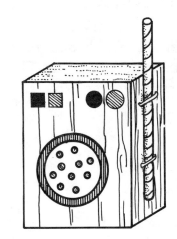

7. WOOD COLLAGES

Have various small pieces of wood available. Let children select pieces of wood and then glue them to heavy cardboard. When the glue is dry, they can paint the collages.

Variation: Let children glue several wood pieces together to produce three-dimensional sculptures. When the glue is dry, they can paint the sculptures.

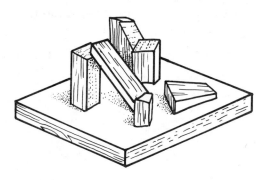

8. WOODEN VEHICLES

Have available a variety of wood pieces for the children to choose from. Let each child experiment with gluing several pieces of wood together to create his or her own vehicle. Aluminum foil can be used for windows. Buttons can be used for wheels. Wooden ice cream spoons can be people in the vehicle. Have markers available so that the children can decorate the people.

9. WORKBENCH CREATIONS

Have various sizes of wood scraps available. Provide hammers, sandpaper, and nails with large heads the first day. Another day, you might want to have a saw, a vise, a tape measure, and glue available at the workbench. Children can create, imagine, invent, and decorate. Make sure an adult is always present to supervise.

 # Dear Parents, Please Save for Me . . .

Aluminum pie tins
Aluminum TV-dinner trays

Beads
Boxes: oatmeal, shoe, cigar, diaper, bandaid, gift
Burlap
Buttons

Canvas
Cartons
Catalogs
Clothespins
Coffee cans
Computer paper
Containers
Corn husks
Costume jewelry
Crayon pieces

Deodorant bottles
Detergent bottles

Egg cartons
Eggshells

Film containers

Gift-wrapping paper
Greeting cards

Junk mail
Keys

Magazines
Material scraps

Microwave dinner containers
Milk cartons: paper, plastic

Newspapers

Paper bags
Pine cones
Pizza boxes
Plastic berry baskets
Plastic bottles
Plastic frozen juice containers

Ribbon

Sandpaper
Seashells
Sheets
Six-pack cartons
Sponges
Spools
Styrofoam cups
Styrofoam packing blocks
Styrofoam packing chips
Styrofoam trays
Supermarket flyers

Toothbrushes (for painting)

Wallpaper books
Wood scraps

Yarn

Materials for Collages and Constructions

Recyclable materials are ideal for collages, constructions, and many other kinds of art projects. Use the list below as a starting point, and then let your imagination be your guide as you build a collection of art materials for your classroom that is full of textures, colors, shapes—and surprises.

Aluminum foil

Bark

Beads: glass, wood

Beans (dried)

Belts: buckles and leather scraps

Blotter paper

Bobby pins and hair clips

Bottles and bottle caps

Boxes and cartons

Braid and rickrack

Broom straws

Buttons

Candles

Cardboard cartons and scraps

Cards: holiday greeting cards, post cards

Carpet scraps

Catalogs: department store, seed and bulb

Chains

Clock parts

Coffee grounds

Corks

Corn husks and kernels

Costume jewelry parts

Cotton puffs

Dowels

Drapery and upholstery samples

Dried flowers, grasses, and seeds

Driftwood

Easter grass

Egg cartons: paper and styrofoam

Eggshells (cleaned)

Elastic

Erasers

Eyelets

Fabric scraps: burlap, felt, oilcloth, silk, velvet, velveteen, wool

Feathers

Film spools and containers

Floor tile and linoleum scraps

Florist's supplies: foam, foil, ribbon, tape, and wire

Flowers: artificial and dried

Food trays: styrofoam, clear plastic, and paper

Fur scraps

Game pieces: checkers, dice, dominoes, and others

Gravel

Inner tube scraps

Junk of any kind

Key rings and tags

Keys

Lace

Leather scraps

Leaves

Lids: jar, spray can, and other small
   containers

Magazines

Marbles

Masonite

Matboard scraps

Mosaic tile

Moss (dried)

Nails

Newspapers

Nuts and bolts

Nuts and nutshells

Paint chips

Paper confetti from paper punches

Paper scraps: construction paper, crepe
   paper, tissue paper

Paper tubes from household goods,
   mailing tubes

Pasta (dry)

Pine cones

Pine needles

Ping-pong balls

Pits: apricot, cherry, peach

Plastic bottles and containers

Popsicle sticks

Rhinestones and costume jewelry "gems"

Ribbons

Rice (uncooked)

Rope pieces

Rubber bands

Sandpaper

Sawdust

Screening

Screws

Seashells

Seeds: acorns (and acorn tops), apple,
   orange, pumpkin, watermelon

Seedpods

Sewing tape: bias tape, seam binding

Shoelaces

Soap

Sponges

Spools

Stamps (cancelled)

Sticks and twigs

Stones and pebbles

String, twine, and cord

Styrofoam chips, packing shapes,
   and trays

Supermarket flyers

Thread: sewing and embroidery

Toothbrushes

Wallpaper samples

Washers

Weeds (dried)

Wire: copper, jewelry, telephone

Wood scraps and shavings

Wheels from toys

Wrapping paper and ribbon

Yarn

Zippers

 # Index of Activities

Classroom Equipment and Supplies

Art Supplies (Styrofoam Trays, 1)

Box Display Case (Boxes, 3)

Bubble Makers (Coffee Cans and Juice Cans, 1)

Building Blocks (Milk Cartons, 5)

Building "Blocks" (Paper Tubes, 3)

Colored Chips (Styrofoam Chips, 3)

Digger (Plastic Bottles, 1)

Feltboard (Boxes, 12)

Funnel (Plastic Bottles, 3)

Giant Blocks (Boxes, 14)

Hollow Blocks (Milk Cartons, 9)

Paint Containers (Coffee Cans and Juice Cans, 8; Milk Cartons, 10)

Paint "Rollers" (Plastic Bottles, 4)

Paint Sets (Egg Cartons, 8)

Playdough Rolling Pins (Paper Tubes, 12)

Printing Blocks (Egg Cartons, 9; Wood Scraps, 4)

Puppet Stage (Boxes, 21)

Sand Play Toys (Paper Tubes, 17)

Scissors Holder (Egg Cartons, 11)

Stencils (Margarine Lids, 8)

Storage Containers (Coffee Cans and Juice Cans, 10; Milk Cartons, 15)

Styrofoam Printing Stamps (Styrofoam Trays, 8)

Table Easel (Boxes, 24)

Texture Paint (Wood Scraps, 5)

Trays for Art Materials (Styrofoam Trays, 9)

Water Play Toys (Margarine Lids, 9; Styrofoam Chips, 16)

Dramatic Play Props

Binoculars (Paper Tubes, 1)

Box Train (Boxes, 5)

Cardboard Vehicles (Paper Tubes, 4)

Cash Register (Boxes, 7)

Doll Bed (Boxes, 9)

Doll House (Boxes, 10; Milk Cartons, 6)

Dramatic Play Props (Plastic Bottles, 2)

Gas Pumps (Boxes, 13)

Grocery Store Props (Coffee Cans and Juice Cans, 6)

Hand Puppets (Fabric, 8)

Imaginary Vehicles (Boxes, 15)

"Instant" Camera (Boxes, 16)

Life-sized Puppets (Boxes, 17)

Masks (Boxes, 18)

Microphones (Paper Tubes, 9)

Playdough Birthday Cakes (Margarine Lids, 6)

Puppets (Paper Tubes, 13)

Shopping Baskets (Boxes, 22)

Stick Puppets (Boxes, 23)

Talking Puppets (Boxes, 25; Egg Cartons, 12)

Teepee (Fabric, 13)

Telephone (Coffee Cans and Juice Cans, 11)

Television (Boxes, 26; Milk Cartons, 16)

Traffic Lights (Milk Cartons, 17)

Two-dimensional Toy Vehicles (Vehicle Brochures, 6)

Vehicle Play Props (Paper Tubes, 21)

Walkie-Talkies (Wood Scraps, 6)

Wooden Vehicles (Wood Scraps, 8)

Games

Bowling Pins (Milk Cartons, 4)

Box Sorting Game (Boxes, 4)

Cereal Box Puzzles (Boxes, 8)

Color Sorting Game (Egg Cartons, 4)

Concentration (Supermarket Flyers, 1)

Egg Carton Game (Egg Cartons, 5)

Fabric Matching Game (Fabric, 6)

Feel and Tell Box (Boxes, 11)

Feely Game (Coffee Cans and Juice Cans, 3)

Fishing Game (Supermarket Flyers, 3)

Food Dominoes (Supermarket Flyers, 4)

Foods Matching Game (Supermarket Flyers, 6)

Foods Sorting Game (Supermarket Flyers, 5)

Garages (Milk Cartons, 8)

Greeting Card Puzzles (Holiday Cards, 2)

Holiday Matching Game (Holiday Cards, 3)

Lotto Game (Supermarket Flyers, 8)

Math Matching Game (Boxes, 19)

Pajamas (Wallpaper, 6)

Pattern Dominoes (Wallpaper, 8)

Pattern Matching Game (Wallpaper, 9)

Plant Containers (Milk Cartons, 11)

Rainy Day Umbrellas (Wallpaper, 11)

Ring Toss Game (Margarine Lids, 7)

Sequencing Game (Coffee Cans and Juice Cans, 9)

Sorting Trays (Styrofoam Trays, 7)

Sound Matching Game (Milk Cartons, 14)

Texture Matching Game (Fabric, 14)

Train Sorting Game (Department Store Catalogs, 3)

Transportation Games (Vehicle Brochures, 4)

Types-of-Travel Sorting Game (Vehicle Brochures, 7)

Vehicle Puzzles (Vehicle Brochures, 9)

Weight Guessing Game (Milk Cartons, 19)

Gift Ideas

Covered Cans (Fabric, 1)

Desk Organizers (Paper Tubes, 6)

Garden Pots (Coffee Cans and Juice Cans, 4)

Gift Containers (Coffee Cans and Juice Cans, 5)

Gift Tags (Holiday Cards, 1)

Holiday Ornaments (Margarine Lids, 2)

Holiday Place Mats (Holiday Cards, 4)

Macaroni Ornaments (Margarine Lids, 3)

Memo Pads (Fabric, 9; Wallpaper, 5)

New Cards (Holiday Cards, 6)

Pencil Holders (Wallpaper, 10)

Pillows (Fabric, 11)

Plastic Candleholders (Plastic Bottles, 5)

"Quilted" Planters (Fabric, 12)

Recipe or Note Holders (Paper Tubes, 14)

Soda Bottle Terrarium (Plastic Bottles, 7)

Vases (Paper Tubes, 20)

Holiday Projects

Christmas Trees (Styrofoam Chips, 2)

Easter Baskets (Milk Cartons, 7)

Gift Tags (Holiday Cards, 1)

Greeting Card Puzzles (Holiday Cards, 2)

Holiday Matching Game (Holiday Cards, 3)

Holiday Ornaments (Margarine Lids, 2)

Holiday Place Mats (Holiday Cards, 4)

Holiday Rubbings (Holiday Cards, 5)

Macaroni Ornaments (Margarine Lids, 3)

New Cards (Holiday Cards, 6)

Salt Cards (Holiday Cards, 7)

Valentine Mailbox (Boxes, 27)

Valentine Mailboxes (Milk Cartons, 18)

Musical Instruments

Drums (Coffee Cans and Juice Cans, 2)

Kazoos (Paper Tubes, 7)

Maracas (Paper Tubes, 8)

Musical Instruments from Wood (Wood Scraps, 3)

Shakers (Milk Cartons, 12)

Reading Activities

Caterpillars (Styrofoam Chips, 1)

Chameleons (Wallpaper, 1)

Inchworms (Styrofoam Chips, 6)

Pajamas (Wallpaper, 6)

Popcorn (Styrofoam Chips, 8)

Train Sorting Game (Department Store Catalogs, 3)

A Truckload of Toys (Department Store Catalogs, 4)

Science Experiments

Mixing Colors Experiment (Egg Cartons, 7)

Science Project: Seed Germination (Egg Cartons, 10)

Science Project: Water Pressure Experiment (Plastic Bottles, 6)

Texture Walk (Styrofoam Chips, 15)

Student Art and Craft Projects

Animal Cages (Magazines, 1)

Art Frames (Boxes, 1)

Art Objects (Egg Cartons, 1)

Barns (Milk Cartons, 1)

Beach Pictures (Styrofoam Trays, 2)

Bird Feeders (Milk Cartons, 2; Paper Tubes, 2)

Boats (Egg Cartons, 2; Milk Cartons, 3; Wood Scraps, 1)

Box Animals (Boxes, 2)

Cages (Boxes, 6)

Carton Animals (Egg Cartons, 3)

Caterpillars (Styrofoam Chips, 1)

Chicks in Eggs (Wallpaper, 2)

Collages (Paper Tubes, 5)

Color Collages (Wallpaper, 3)

Dip and Dye Fabric (Fabric, 2)

Fabric Animals and People (Fabric, 3)

Fabric Collages (Fabric, 4)

Fabric Flowers (Fabric, 5)

Fabric Mobiles (Margarine Lids, 1)

Fabric Painting (Fabric, 7)

Face Collages (Styrofoam Chips, 4)

Faces (Magazines, 2)

Favorite Foods Collage (Supermarket Flyers, 2)

Fingerpaint Prints (Styrofoam Trays, 3)

Fish (Wallpaper, 4)

Flowers (Egg Cartons, 6)

Geoboards (Wood Scraps, 2)

Grocery Mural (Supermarket Flyers, 7)

Houses (Department Store Catalogs, 1)

Igloos (Styrofoam Chips, 5)

Inchworms (Styrofoam Chips, 6)

Magic Paint (Coffee Cans and Juice Cans, 7)

Mobiles (Margarine Lids, 4; Paper Tubes, 10)

Monoprints (Styrofoam Trays, 4)

Necklaces (Margarine Lids, 5; Paper Tubes, 11)

Number Collages (Styrofoam Chips, 7; Supermarket Flyers, 9)

Our Town (Boxes, 20)

Pack Your Suitcase (Department Store Catalogs, 2)

Paper Chains (Wallpaper, 7)

Parachutes (Fabric, 10)

Picture Books (Vehicle Brochures, 1)

Popcorn (Styrofoam Chips, 8)

Pussy Willows (Styrofoam Chips, 9)

Robots (Paper Tubes, 15)

Rockets (Paper Tubes, 16)

Sculptures (Styrofoam Chips, 10)

Sewing Cards (Holiday Cards, 8; Styrofoam Trays, 5)

Shapes (Styrofoam Chips, 11)

Ships (Styrofoam Trays, 6)

Shopping Carts (Supermarket Flyers, 10)

Shopping Lists (Supermarket Flyers, 11)

Simple Houses (Milk Cartons, 13)

Snakes (Paper Tubes, 18)

Snowballs (Styrofoam Chips, 12)

Snow Necklaces (Styrofoam Chips, 13)

Sparkly Collages (Styrofoam Chips, 14)

Story Starters: "My Trip" (Vehicle Brochures, 2)

Strip Collages (Wallpaper, 12)

Stripe Collages (Wallpaper, 13)

Stuffed Fish (Wallpaper, 14)

Theme Collages (Magazines, 3)

"Things That Go" Collage (Vehicle Brochures, 3)

Transportation Mural (Vehicle Brochures, 5)

A Truckload of Toys (Department Store Catalogs, 4)

Tube Art (Paper Tubes, 19)

Turtles (Egg Cartons, 13)

Vehicle Mobiles (Vehicle Brochures, 8)

Windsocks (Fabric, 15)

Wood Collages (Wood Scraps, 7)

Workbench Creations (Wood Scraps, 9)

Yarn Weaving (Styrofoam Trays, 10)